And Gone Tomorrow

Andrew J. Offutt

Alpha Editions

This Edition Published in 2021

ISBN: 9789355348517

Design and Setting By
Alpha Editions
www.alphaedis.com
Email – info@alphaedis.com

Here is the best story submitted in answer to the theme question: "What Will Life in America Be Like 100 Years From Now?" ... Written by an undergraduate at the University of Louisville, Louisville, Kentucky, it pictures the America of 2054 as part of a world empire run by an Italian dictator and very similar to that of the ancient Caesars and the early Roman Empire. There is one language, one religion and customs and laws have changed to suit the times. But, basically, human nature hasn't changed and there is the omnipresent clash of faction against faction. The theme is that a dictatorship is the only perfect form of government. If there is a moral, it is that there is no permanent form of government.

One of the requirements for entering IF's College Science Fiction Contest was that the contestant be a "simon pure" amateur—never having been published professionally. This is Andy Offut's first published story, and it has been accorded the same editing we give to professional manuscripts. No rewriting or revisions have been made. See November IF for complete announcement of this and the six other winners in this nation-wide contest.

He sat down suddenly. He stared up at the man.

"Say it again," he muttered.

He knew what the answer would be even before the man repeated it in that quiet voice.

"This is June 3, 2054."

The fellow wasn't kidding him. He was serious enough. But a couple of minutes ago it had been May 15, 1954. He looked at his watch and grunted. Less than four minutes ago it had been 1954. Reality. Now it was June 3, 2054. There were four steel walls. There was a steel chair. There were no windows.

He tried to take it calmly. But the unbelievable horror of being *where* he was and *when* he was and the man calmly repeating, "This is June 3, 2054," screamed for release.

"No! No! You're lying! It's impossible!" He grabbed the man's tunic and drew back a doubled fist. His chair went over behind him.

Then a stiff thumb jabbed him in the short ribs and he grunted and went down.

"This is June 3, 2054. You are still in Louisville, Kentucky. You are standing in a room adjoining the laboratory in the Time Building on 3rd Street at Eastern Parkway. This is the receiving room. My name is Kevin Ilaria. You've come through time. Is that so impossible to grasp? You're a thinking man. Educated!"

He looked up from the floor.

"Well?"

"So I'm a thinking man and an educated man. And what happens? I'm sapped. I'm shanghaied. I'm walking down Confederate Place to my old fraternity house at 1:00 in the morning. I've just had a row with my girl. I'm heading for the fraternity house to see who'll go down to Herman's and get good and drunk with me. And somebody clobbers me. The next thing I remember I'm sitting in a steel chair in a steel room without any windows. Just like this one. There's a man standing there. A man with watery, myopic eyes under bushy brows and his hair parted in the middle. He's Doctor Borley, of the University of Louisville Chemistry Department. There's another man with him. A little fellow with thick glasses and a crew cut and eyes like the slits between closed Venetian blinds. He's Doctor Schink, of the Psychology Department. They're talking about me."

"Umn hmn. Now you're beginning to sound normal. Doctors Borley and Schink are our agents in 1954. Do you know where you were?"

"I told you. In some sort of steel room without win—"

The man made an impatient gesture with his hand. "No, I mean *where*. You were in a steel chamber in the Daynolds Metals Plant. It stood on this spot in 1954. Two people knew—know—about that room."

"Doctor Borley and Doctor Schink?"

"I'm glad you've calmed down. Now we can talk."

Jay wasn't quite ready to calm down. "You stand there in that Roman outfit and talk about being calm. To me. To me, Jay Welch, a history major who took his AB from the University of Louisville in 1950. Jay Welch, average guy, who got into an average argument with the girl he pinned in 1950 and went for a walk to drown his sorrows and wound up one hundred years from where—when—he started. I—"

"Then you admit you've come through Time?"

"I may as well."

Ilaria cursed quietly. "But you're not an average guy. You have a working knowledge of chemistry and biology and physics and history and a few arts and sociology and psychology and geopolitics and literature and the English language as spoken in AD 1954. You hope to be successful as a writer. You're Public Relations Consultant with Duo-Point, one of the biggest corporations in your nation in 1954."

"Yes," Jay Welch said. "And I make good money. Even better than a bus driver or a steam-fitter. So?"

"So here you are. 1954's representative to 2054." Ilaria was only a man. He could not keep the flourish and the Hollywood grandeur out of his voice.

"Yes! And what happens tomorrow when I don't show up for work? What happens in a few days when people find out I've disappeared? What happens when they find out Julie was the last person I was with? What—"

"You're getting yourself worked up again, Jay Welch. Don't you think we have thought of those things? We've brought you across one hundred years, Jay Welch."

"Yes," Jay said quietly, flatly. "Yes." Then just as flatly, just as quietly he said, "Why?"

"So you've remembered to wonder about that at last." Ilaria smiled. Jay noticed that the smile was one-sided and pulled back the left corner of Ilaria's mouth. He stood there and looked down at Jay Welch, who had forgotten that he was sitting on the floor. His tunic was white and there were three diamond-shaped silver pieces in a vertical line on each elbow-length sleeve. There was a wide blue stripe and a narrow silver stripe at the hem of his tunic and at his sleeves. He wore sandals. His belt was leather and there was a holstered pistol of some sort hanging at his left hip. In tiny blue script above his left breast pocket were the words 'Trib. Ilaria'. On the pocket was a red disk with the letters PR. A silver-worked blue cloak was flung over his shoulders. Except for the identification and the odd fabric of his clothes and the holstered gun he looked very like a young Roman of the first century.

Ilaria's slow smile pulled back the left corner of his mouth. "Because you are who you are and what you are. Because you attended the University of Louisville and Doctors Borley and Schink knew you. Because they chose you. Merely because they chose you. They might've chosen anyone else.

"We've your personality pretty well mapped out. We expected violence. That's why I'm here. I'm a psychologist and an anthropologist. I'm a fast-talker and I can convince people and place them at ease. I'm also big enough to handle you, Jay Welch."

From his position on the floor Jay looked up at Ilaria and decided the man from 2054 was big enough. Jay Welch was six feet one inch tall. He weighed one seventy-three and wore a 40-long suit. Kevin Ilaria was bigger.

Jay was forced to grin. The tall blond man was a likeable guy, at that. A human being.

"Who are you?"

"Kevin Ilaria. Doctor of Psychology. That entitles me to the silver band on my tunic. Also a Tribune. That entitles me to the blue stripe and the three silver diamonds and the gun."

"A Tribune? In what? Of what?"

"In the Forces. In the actual ranks, a Tribune commands 7,000 men, 250 planes or a base, or 40 tanks. But I've never had a chance to go into the field. There has been no cause to fight. Meantime I'm stationed at Standiford Field as second-in-command. A friend of mine named Rinaldi fills in for me. He's a Sub-Tribune.

"I've been specializing in the study of Time."

"The way you say Time it sounds as though it were capitalized. Where I come from Time with a capital T is a magazine."

Kevin Ilaria laughed. He reached down a hand. "Get up," he said, and, taking Jay's forearm, helped him to his feet.

"Let's go," he said.

Jay didn't bother to ask where they were going. He followed the Tribune out the door and into the hall. On the wall just outside the door, was a black box. Two squares cut into it shone with a faint white light. Ilaria paused and shielded the lighted areas a moment with his hand, and Jay saw the light go out in the room they had just left. Ilaria closed the door. As he turned, Jay saw the white letters PR emblazoned on the back of his cloak.

"This way," he said. Jay noticed that Ilaria walked on his right, so that the Tribune's gun was between them.

"The way I said Time, it *is* capitalized. It means all the Time since the beginning. It's a corporation, like your Duo-Point. Only much larger, and much less known. Our job is to learn."

"That's a big order," Jay commented. "You learn by—borrowing—emissaries?"

Ilaria laughed again. "Thanks for the phraseology, but it wouldn't worry me if you called it 'kidnaping' or 'shanghaiing.' You're right, of course. We learn by sending men from this age to other ones, and by pulling men from other ages to this one. Doctor Schink is our Emissary to 1954. His real name is Clyde Gabrinaldi. Borley is our contact there ... rather, then."

"Well I'll be damned! I've gone to Clyde a lot of times for advice."

The left corner of Ilaria's mouth pulled back as his grin widened. "Umn hmn. He's married, too. With a child. He's there for good."

Jay was afraid to ask if emissaries from the past to 2054 were "there for good" too. He changed the subject.

"You started to tell me before—"

"Oh, yes. I'm to be your teacher and companion. But I'll try to give you a quick fill-in. Our world of 2054 is quite different from yours. And, we hope, in better shape. We've proved that the only way to maintain world peace is by world government. And the only successful type of government is a dictatorship."

Jay gasped. "You mean the entire world—has reverted to *dictatorship?*"

Ilaria laughed. "Not *reverted*. We finally accepted it as the only logical form of government for an entire world."

"What happens when the dictator goes wild? He always has."

The smile was there again. "You're not quite ready for that," Ilaria told him. "But, it has been taken into consideration."

Out of the corner of his eye, Jay saw the slight puff of Ilaria's chest, the self-satisfied square of his shoulders, the quick set of his jaw. He wondered what part Tribune Kevin Ilaria played in the 'dictator control' this world had provided.

"The system has worked and is working. See this?"

They turned a corner in the corridor and faced a great domed room. On the far wall hung a white tapestry of something like 40 x 40 foot dimensions. On it, emblazoned in letters of red and yellow made to look like flame, were the characters PPB. In the lower right-hand corner, in white outlined with blue, was the same PR that Ilaria wore. Jay waited for the Tribune's explanation.

"PpB stands for Pax per Bello," Ilaria explained. "Peace through War. That slogan was written in 1967 by Julius and adapted in 1971 as official."

"Julius?"

"Yes. The first Dictator."

Things were beginning to click in Jay's mind.

"I think I know what PR stands for," he said. "Pax Romana."

As always, Ilaria smiled. "That's right," he said.

The command-car marked with the PR symbol pulled over and stopped.

"What is it? Who are you?" the driver demanded.

The Captain on the seat beside him peered into the blackness and cursed.

The man who had waved the vehicle to a halt walked away.

"Here!" the Captain cried. "What in blazes is going on here? Why'd you stop us? Centurion! Stop that man!"

The two Centurions in the back seat looked at the Captain for a moment, then they both jumped out and ran after the man.

An ellipsoidal grey thing streaked out of the darkness, landed in the driver's lap and thudded to the floor of the car. The Captain threw open his door and started to climb out. The driver bent over to see what it was.

At that moment the driver, the command-car and the Captain blew up.

The silence that followed was broken by the blast of a submachine gun as it struck down the two centurions.

"Take their weapons," said a brittle voice.

The detachment of soldiers from the garrison at Tel Aviv stopped and looked around.

"Sir, what is it?" asked a guard anxiously.

"Terribly quiet out here; something's up," the Lieutenant muttered calmly.

There were seven of them. The Lieutenant, the Centurion, and five legionaries. They had grown accustomed to the quiet life of garrison men in a calm, conquered city. When there is nothing tangible to be guarded, a guard's life is a dull one. The guns they carried were the symbol of their authority, and had never been used for any other purpose.

They looked around. The dirty, once-white buildings rose close on either side. There was no moon. There was no sound. The darkness and the silence could have been cut with a knife.

The Lieutenant grinned. He didn't feel much like grinning. He spoke. He didn't feel much like talking, either.

"This darkness is thick," he said. "You could cut it with a knife. Wish I had a knife."

He got a knife. The men had just started to laugh when the Lieutenant got it.

Between his shoulder blades.

As the Lieutenant toppled forward, the Centurion dodged close against the dirty stone wall and yelled "Spread out!"

They killed a lot of the shadowy, green-clad attackers, but there were only six of them and they were cornered. When the enemy drove a tank into the alley and sprayed them with its mounted gun they died.

"Take their weapons," said a quiet voice.

The half-track rolled to a stop.

"Where, Sir?" the driver wanted to know.

"Beyond that big crater over there. The sun glinted on metal. I'm sure of it. Didn't you see it?"

"No, Sir." The driver craned his neck. There was nothing but barren rubble and bomb craters and torn, twisted metal and ruined buildings.

"There are all sorts of old automobiles lying around out there, Sir," the driver volunteered.

"Yes, and they've been here long enough to get good and rusty," the Captain snapped. "This is something else."

The driver craned his neck. There was nothing but rubble.

Eight men in the back of the half-track leaped to their feet when they heard the faint clicking of KCN-H2SO4 guns and the buzz of an old gamma gun and the sharp bark of a very old sub machine-gun. But a grenade landed on the truck and another rolled under it.

Another wreck was added to the rubble.

"Take their weapons, if there are any left," said a quiet voice.

And in the more peaceful city of Louisville, Jay Welch was introduced to Kevin Ilaria's best friend, his adjutant at Standiford Field.

Jay took a liking to Sub-Tribune Jason Rinaldi the moment he felt the fellow's firm grip.

"Jason is adjutant," Ilaria explained. "And one of the few 'field soldiers' who manages to get along with Caesar's Pretorian Prefect, Lamberti. How he does it, I don't know. Lamberti's absolutely unbearable."

"Prejudice. Middle-class prejudices," Rinaldi grinned. He was short and very dark with a lot of black hair.

Ilaria's left cheek cracked into a long dimple as he smiled. "He picks on me because I'm a serious psychologist."

Rinaldi laughed. "As a psychologist, Kevin, you're an excellent bridge player. As a soldier—"

"Just remember who's got three bars and who has two."

Rinaldi waved his hand and shrugged. "They pass 'em out to psych boys wholesale," he said, and ducked Ilaria's swing. "Slow reflexes, too," he added as he turned to go.

Ilaria stopped him at the door and murmured a few sentences.

Jay caught something about sabotage at Standiford. Rinaldi seemed to be attributing it to the Commanding Officer there.

"Nice guy," Jay said as the door closed behind Rinaldi.

"You said it. Good officer, too. He'll root out the bird who's playing around out there. Can't figure out why it's being done."

"Factions," Jay said, "—within factions."

"Little ones always exist, I guess. Have you finished with the history films?"

"I've seen them, yes. I'm still trying to digest them."

"The language give you much trouble?"

"Quite a bit, but I think I got most of it.

"One man," Jay went on wonderingly. "One man. A Captain in the Italian Army.

"The Communist forces in Indo-China had been driven back and Captain—then Major—Lollabrigida went in after them.

"The defeat was becoming so terrible that the Kremlin dealt itself a playing hand rather than the dummy it had been playing. Red forces came piling in. Lollabrigida and his Italian troops stopped them cold. Then he seemed to sway. And, when the Commies pounced for the kill, they were trapped, pocketed, and annihilated.

"American newspapers and commentators began to call Major Julius Lollabrigida 'Julius Caesar.' Italy became big overnight. The Big Three became Russia, the United States, and Italy. Lollabrigida appealed to America—sometime in there they made him a Colonel, but he was actually telling the Generals and the Italian government what to do—for aid in going ahead aggressively.

"And America turned him down. They were still playing 'wait and see.' They waited. They waited too long. The Commies got tired of waiting around and sent a couple of jet bombers with A-bombs."

"Now you're telling me things," Ilaria interrupted. "I'm pretty shady on that period myself."

Jay shrugged. "It was after my time. All I know is what the films show. Two planes, each with a seven-man crew, and each carrying one atomic bomb, were dispatched from an airbase somewhere near Juneau." Jay stopped.

"And?"

The man from 1954 choked. It was hard to be objective about this. It wasn't so easy for him to pass off as the film had done.

"And—" he hesitated.

"It's over, Jay. It's done with. It doesn't even concern you anymore. It belongs to a past era."

"One was headed for New York. The other struck farther inland ... for Washington. The first one was shot down by an F-117 border patrol plane. The other one got through. It—it levelled the capitol.

Almost completely. The White House and the Pentagon were destroyed."

Ilaria sat quietly and waited. Jay didn't go on.

"Thus removing the United States of America, as such, from a prominent position in the world picture," Ilaria said.

"Yes. I can't understand it. Everything just folded up. SAC didn't even get off the ground. And Colonel Lollabrigida, by then Commander-in-Chief of the UN forces, sent fifty planes, each with one A-bomb, over the Kremlin. One was shot down over Vladivostok, but the bombardier pulled the firing pin as the ship crashed and most of Vladivostok was destroyed. Six other planes made it to their destinations and dropped their loads. I can't remember the cities ... one was a new super airbase near Moscow. Five of the planes returned. None had managed to reach Moscow. Half the world was in ruins. The Pope begged that the War be stopped."

Ilaria snorted. "He knew they'd hit Rome!"

Jay looked at him. "Is that what you think?"

Ilaria shrugged and flashed that quick, winning smile. "There are no other motives, are there?"

Jay stared. What changes had taken place in religious philosophy in this hard-bitten world of 2054?

Kevin Ilaria shrugged, smiling. "That's unimportant. Let's go on with the history lesson. Then what?"

"Uh—oh, yes. As I remember Julius Lollabrigida, to be trite, launched an 'all-out offensive' against Communist forces everywhere. People were afraid of Russia, but they were afraid of Lollabrigida and Rome, too. So they joined him. Aid poured into the UN. Czechoslovakia was taken and Poland and Hungary and finally only the old Russia of pre World War II days was left. And in they went.

"Then Lollabrigida's saboteurs exploded an atomic bomb in the heart of Moscow. After that it was pretty easy sledding."

"Astounding how a nation seems to fall apart when its capitol and its leaders are gone," Ilaria remarked.

"Everybody and everything folds," Jay said. "Morale dies.

"After the demolition of Moscow and other parts of the USSR, Italy stood at the top. General of the Armies Julius Lollabrigida marched back into Italy and into Rome and into the capitol and up on a pedestal. He stood as Italy's utter ruler. His last name was lost and replaced by 'Caesar II.' He was named Dictator.

"From mighty Rome, Caesar sent out linguists and anthropologists and ethnologists and psychologists and military men and others. In twenty years, twenty peaceful years, Italian had become the language of the world. A few minor uprisings in America and in Japan were smashed. Julius Caesar II was World Dictator of the Republic of Earth. Someone in America denied him and was torn to pieces by the people. Someone in Italy spread literature of dissension and was hunted down and liquidated by Caesar's personal police, the Pretoriani. And so it went.

"Caesar adopted a prominent Air Force Colonel who became Caesar III on Lollabrigida's death. Each year on his birthday men were silent. No business was transacted. No one left his home. Except blue-and-silver clad soldiers, wearing PR armbands. Caesar's Pretorians. No one *dared* venture out.

"During the reign of Caesar III, every person in the world changed his last name to an Italian one. The Ali bens and the Chicos and the Andres and the Fritzes and the Johns became Marianos and Roccos and Caldinis and Campisanos and diManos."

There was silence for a moment.

"The thing I can't understand," Jay mused, "is why in all these years there hasn't been a 'bad' Caesar, or an uprising."

"What do you mean by 'bad' Caesar?"

Jay shrugged. "In the first Pax Romana there was Caligula, who was insane. Nero, who preferred artistic diversions to politics. There was Galba, who didn't know what was going on. And so on. And on and on. Your three dictators so far seem to have done excellent jobs. They seem to be damned conscientious leaders."

"When you re-create something," Ilaria told him, "you try to eliminate its faults."

"Of course. But what if Caesar's son or a Caesar's adopted son goes bad?" Jay elucidated.

"So far we haven't had that problem to deal with. But we're ready. Each time a new Dictator comes to power, one thousand top military men draw folded pieces of plastipaper from a 'bowl.' On twenty of these are X's. The others contain O's. The twenty X's are a secret organization, sworn to kill the Dictator if it should become necessary. When Caesar, as you say, 'goes bad'."

"Brilliant!" Jay breathed. "And he—Caesar—never knows who they are?"

"*No* one ever knows," Ilaria said. "Not even the members. They remain in contact, but none ever knows who the others are."

Jay remembered Ilaria's previous mention of the system, and the unconscious swelling of the Tribune's chest at the time. "You're one," he said.

Ilaria was caught off guard. "I—yes," he said. "I won't ask how you knew."

"A guess. Then you've been a—whatever it's called—for nine years, during Caesar V's reign."

"That's right."

"And you don't know any of the others?"

"Only one. I found out accidentally. He—" Ilaria stopped.

Jay shrugged. "I won't ask any more questions along that line," he promised. "But I still can't believe there haven't been any uprisings!"

"None. Caesar II died of a heart attack. Caesar III had a brain tumor which we learned about too late. His son never had a chance to prove himself, other than that he was brave and foolish. He swam the Rubicon at its widest point, then walked to Rome in his shorts in the dead of winter. He died of pneumonia. Caesar V, our Dictator today, is strong and quiet. He holds the Empire firmly unified. But he does nothing extraordinary. And he is too lenient."

"I just can't conceive of such perfection!"

Kevin Ilaria smiled. He walked over to the window and peered out. "*You* couldn't. But this *is* the perfect government. Everyone is satisfied. One ruler. One capitol. One army. One language. One nationality. One world. One religion."

"I realize—" Jay halted. "One religion?" he demanded.

"Yes."

"What is it?" He found himself afraid of the answer. The indications were there, in plain sight. He guessed it before Kevin Ilaria turned from the window and said:

"Caesarism."

The man called Gaius Julius Caesar Imperator V turned from the window and rubbed his hand over his graying hair.

"This is the first time I've ever run into anything of this sort."

The President of the Senate shrugged. He was an old man who had been placed in the Senate by his father in 1980. So long ago that people wondered when he would die. They were tired of these old men dictating to their ruler, as many people before them had been tired. The rise of the President of the Senate to leadership of that revered group had not been meteoric by any means. But his maintenance of the position had been tenacious. He was a careful man.

The President of the Senate shrugged. "It is. It is the first time anything of this sort has ever come up, Julius. Therefore it is up to you to set an example."

Caesar glanced over at General Bonadella. The General nodded in agreement with Senator Chianti.

"This sort of business can break up the Empire if it's allowed to continue, Caesar," he said, in his pompous military way. "I say death."

Major DeCosta nodded quietly.

"Thumbs down all around, is it?" Caesar sat down behind his desk and picked up the speaker of his private cable to London. He looked at the three men.

"Commander in charge of Garrison C," he said.

There was a silent moment.

They looked up as Prefect Lamberti of the Pretorians, the Imperial personal bodyguard (it had progressed far beyond that. Its enrollment was tremendous; its power second only to the Dictator's) came in. The Senator nodded. The two field soldiers turned quickly away. The men of the field did not get along with the Pretorian dandies.

"Commander? This is the Dictator," Caesar said unnecessarily. The garrison commander knew that only one person could call him on that line. The phone would react to no voice other than Caesar's.

"Have you the fellow who was preaching dissension? I say one year in prison. You heard me. Yes, one year. What? No! No torture!" He severed connections and looked up at his advisers.

Prefect Lamberti shook his head. Senator Chianti turned and stalked out. After a moment General Bonadella followed. The Major turned away to stare out the window. He shook his head.

"del Ponta? This is the Dictator," that quiet, flat voice said behind him. Caesar was calling the under-chief of the Pretoriani. "I will speak tomorrow from the balcony. Yes. 1400. Of course. World-wide. That's right. Oh, I suppose about a quarter 'til."

The man who ruled the world stood up and stared at Major DeCosta's back. At forty-one, Caesar was a gaunt man with stooped shoulders and sad lines running from his nostrils to the corners of his mouth. His forehead was lined and re-lined, and the keen brown eyes were dulled with years of decisions and hard work.

He was tired.

They called him the Hound because his face bore the same sad, quiet look worn by those dogs. And they called him weak because he let offenders off too easily.

DeCosta turned around. The young Major met his Chief's gaze.

"Well?" The voice of the Dictator was quiet and calm.

DeCosta's eyes flickered. He straightened militarily. He shrugged.

"It is not for me to say, Sir."

A slow smile spread over those weary features. "And you, Farouk?"

Lamberti stretched out his arm and balled his fist with the thumb extended and pointing down. "You know me, Caesar."

"I do. Even my best friend disagrees with my decisions now, after all these years of elbow-rubbing.

"You are usually more out-spoken, Major DeCosta. Have you nothing more to say?"

DeCosta's reply was slow in coming but rapid in delivery. "I am around Caesar much of late," he rapped out. His back was stiff and military as he strode out of the Dictator's office.

Prefect Lamberti's gloved hand dropped to the butt of his gun, but Caesar shook his head in gentle negation.

Julius Caesar Imperator V gazed sadly at the closed door.

Jay had given up trying to reason with Ilaria about God. The man was intelligent as well as brilliant—there's a tremendous difference—about everything else, but he was stubbornly obstinate to Jay's arguments. At least in Jay's terminology he was stubbornly obstinate. All faith is stubborn obstinacy. Kevin Ilaria's faith was appalling. His arguments were beautiful. Flawless. Jay thought of his old friend, Father O'mare. Even that great psychologist-priest would be hard-put, he decided.

So he quit. He didn't give up. He just quit.

Can you tell a man the Earth's flat after he's been up in a jet?

Can you talk a bullet out of pursuing its path?

Can you reason with a Marxist?

"If a man can conquer the greatest enemy the world has ever faced, is he not God? If he can turn from killing and soldiering to soothing and pacifying, is he not God? If he can make the world one, after twenty-two centuries of 'world anarchism' is he not God? If he can maintain the peace and keep the people happy and heal all sores is he not God? If he just looks at you when you call him 'God' or 'Savior' and smiles and say 'I?' is he not God? If he chooses the perfect man to continue in his place, is he not God?"

"But that's proof! Why die? Isn't God immortal?"

"Only God could realize that one man can't continue to reign indefinitely. His ideas, yes. But he must create another to carry on his ideas. There must be variety and diversions."

Unshakeable. Unquestioning. Jay could never understand a person's sticking to the claim 'I'm a Christian' or 'I'm a Moslem' when he would be killed for it. Jay had always figured he'd have said to Nero's men 'Me? Me? A filthy Christian? Not I. I love Jupiter and Juno. Step inside and see my altars ...'

Now he was seeing what sturdy, rock-firm martyr faith was like.

So he quit.

Instead he learned about the gyro-jet cars which hugged the roads like lovers on a honeymoon. He watched them sprout stubby wings and breathe flame and soar straight up. He learned about saying 'Open' to a lock and having the electronic device 'recognize' him and let him in. He learned about personalphones which 'recognized' your voice. He learned about the tiny pellet of potassium cyanide and sulphuric acid with which the guns were loaded. The pellets struck and broke and the victim was dead in seconds. Very humane. No maimed or wounded. Just the dead.

He learned about self-shaping sandals—the most comfortable and most sensible shoes man had ever worn—and air baths and soft-voiced alarm clocks which politely told you it was time to get up and about unbreakable ring-finger chronos and about atomic heating and flawless plumbing and he saw plastic, plastic, plastic.

He learned about all of them. But his real delight was the depilatory cream. This, above all others, was man's greatest invention.

"No shaving ... no silly damned socks or tight, hot shoes or tie ... no battery stalling or flat tires ... I guess this is paradise, Kevin!"

"And the perfect government and the perfect religion! All one race! One religion! One nation! One language! One nationality! One God!" Ilaria added exuberantly.

"That reminds me. How come I never see any coloreds?"

"Haven't you? By the way, no murderous car insurance or alimony laws, either. And no need for them. All marriages are ideal."

Jay was readily detoured to this new novelty.

"Now, don't let's go too far. Identical religion and race and customs and ideals and opinions may lower the divorce rate a lot, but there's still ye olde sex angle. A couple can go together twenty years and break up on the wedding night. Some are hot and some are cold and some are slow and some are fast. The only thing you could have improved on, is sex education. It's astounding how many people of my time know nothing about the sexual part of marriage. The most important part!

"Of course it's doing what comes naturally; but what if two people have been taught from different viewpoints? Or if one hasn't been taught at all? Some people are actually ashamed or embarrassed. There are intelligent people who don't even know the biological facts! Few—especially women, know about the pleasure and the habit-forming angle. That's the one thing than can break up something beautiful in ten minutes.

"Education, maybe. Human nature, no."

"Whew!"

"Excuse me, Kevin, for launching into a Phillipic, but that's long been my pet peeve. Atrocious, deplorable, and all that."

"We don't *usually* tamper with human nature, Jay. As a rule, that is. This is going to come as a shock to you, with your silly, 'atrocious and deplorable' 1954 ideas and morals.

"A trial period. A pre-marital period of living together for a couple of weeks. If the couple isn't sexually suited, they either attempt to have it remedied by a physician or break off."

"A shock, yes," Jay murmured, slowly shaking his head. "How did it ever start? Anyone who'd propound an idea like that in my time would be accused of being some sort of perverted sex-fiend!

"A foolproof, flawless plan to insure happy marriages!"

Half across the world a door swung open and a tall dark man with piercing black eyes and a twin-tufted beard came in. His dark-green garment, faintly resembling a trench-coat, was double-breasted and belted and military cut. His feet were encased in plastileather boots which clicked as he came to attention before the desk.

The plate on the desk read "Praefectus Praetoriani."

"Major del Ponta, Sir."

The man behind the desk looked up. "At ease, Major."

Major Ali ben del Ponta relaxed and waited.

The man behind the desk finished scanning the sheet of micro-paper, marked something on it with a stylo, stuck it in the pneumatube on the corner of his desk, and pushed the button to close his desk drawer. He looked up at Major Ali ben del Ponta.

"Well?" He put his hands together, fingers touching.

"It has begun, Prefect Lamberti. All over the world our local men are leading their followers in attack. Captain Abram Mazzoli has sent in his report from Tel Aviv. The city is in his hands. Captain Mahomet DiSanto's 'Raiders' have complete control of the Sahara. Captain Arnaldi's forces are firmly entrenched in the old Washington area of America. He will move northward to meet Colonel Magnani's forces from Canada and Commander Campisano. They—"

"Campisano's airborne ready to roll?"

"Yes, Sir. Arrangements have been made. The drop will be just outside New York."

"Alright. Then everything has gone off as scheduled?"

"Yes, Sir."

Prefect Farouk Lamberti regarded his deskchron thoughtfully.

"And Caesar will make his speech in twenty-five hours and thirty-three minutes?"

Major del Ponta glanced at his own chron, which was strapped to the third finger of his left hand. "Yes, Sir. At 1400, tomorrow."

"Have the twenty-foot 'visor screen activated for public showing. Mount it outside as we'd planned."

"It's being taken care of, Sir. The screen is on its way to the Square. There will be a crowd."

"Good. We all want to hear noble Caesar."

Del Ponta grinned. "Yes, Sir. We all do. Especially tomorrow."

"He doesn't know?—or suspect?"

"He shouldn't Sir. Our men took over and began covering up at once. You know the atrocious condition of world communications systems. The Empire could fall and Rome might not hear of it for days."

"That's what I was counting on ... that and the Disturber. The degeneracy of the field military is terrible. They are allowing themselves to get lazy and fat and careless."

"Yes, Sir."

"Have my car ready to drive to the Square behind Caesar's tomorrow. See that the covermen in the houses around the Square are doubled and double-checked. But when we go to the show, let's not have too great an exhibition of Imperial power. We don't want this thing to backfire and cut our own throats."

"Yes, Sir." Del Ponta's grin widened.

"Dismissed."

Del Ponta came to attention, saluted and about-faced and left.

Prefect Lamberti opened his desk drawer and took out his old service pistol. It was a gamma gun. He had not released any of the deadly, slow-acting rays from its chamber in seven years. But it was ready.

He opened another drawer and took out a white cloak, marked across the back with a blue dove and the single word 'Liberacione.'

He checked the pistol.

"Does the Emissary from 1954 get to meet Caesar?" Jay wanted to know.

"Later. He's to make a speech tomorrow afternoon. It will be world-televised."

"He looks very old and very tired," Jay ventured. He'd seen Caesar on transcriptions of old speeches and on old newsreels.

"He's about ... forty, I think. Somewhat weak. Very lenient."

"I would've guessed him to be a good deal older." Then "Why weak? Because he's lenient?"

Ilaria smiled. "Remember, Jay, 'Pax per Bello.' Too much leniency leads one's subjects to be bold. Over-bold."

"One man's opinion?"

The Tribune shrugged. "No. Caesar doesn't get along with his advisors too well. They criticize him for being too ready to forgive and forget."

The more Jay saw of this perfect world, the more he realized how cruel and hard people must be to maintain a paradise. If everyone is to be happy, someone must be unhappy.

The trouble is, people don't like to be told "This is for your own good."

Jay said so.

"But if they're sat on hard enough," Ilaria rebutted, "they don't have a chance ever to try anything else which they might *think* is for their own good...."

Jay nodded. Very true. As Ilaria left the room Jay went to the window and looked out at the Louisville of 2054. For the millionth time in the seven days he'd been here, he wished he had a cigarette. They had been outlawed as detrimental to health long ago.

The fact that it had been seven days reminded him of something else left behind.

Julie.

"You're a fool," he finally told himself. No wonder Julie'd been on edge and acting what he termed 'odd' lately! She was scared. He'd been out of school three and a half years. He was twenty-five. He'd just bought a new Olds. He'd begun buying his clothes at *The* Store rather than a store. Hell, he should've been married long ago. His days here were full. There were meetings with scientists and historians and militarists and linguists and everyone else Kevin could think up. He talked and listened and discussed and lectured. But he thought of her every night. Every morning before he rose. At times like this, when he was alone for a few minutes.

Of course it was love! He'd always thought too many people threw the word around too much. He'd always been afraid to use it because he wasn't sure of its meaning. He's used it once. And he'd been kicked in the teeth by the girl. He hadn't used it since.

When was a guy ever sure?

Hogwash! Now he knew that each man forms his own definition. True, too many people used the word love indiscriminately. It's mistreated. Kicked around. Assumed and taken off. Dragged through messes and scandals and law courts and through the mud. But to a man like Jay Welch, to a man who has been afraid—yes, afraid—to use it, it *must* be there when he begins thinking in those terms.

Love. He'd had to come across one-hundred years to realize he'd found its meaning. To realize he'd known its meaning a long time. To realize that love is whatever you make it, what you, yourself, call it. You define it yourself. Then you apply it.

It had been there all the time. You don't include someone in everything you do and everything you think without it. You don't try to change her and yourself. To make her perfect. To make yourself perfect with—and for—her without it. This business about "accepting" little faults—as well as big ones—, he decided, is for the birds. It's human nature to translate other people in terms of yourself and try to change them in terms of yourself. To argue and be proud and hate like hell to have to make up. But you don't make a project of it with everyone. Not unless....

He and Julie had a lot to talk about.

Then he remembered where he was and when he was. He thought of Doctor Schink. And suddenly he was scared. He remembered what Ilaria had said about Schink. 'He's there for good....'

"He's never said a word about my going back!"

"Neither have you," came Ilaria's voice, and Jay whirled around to see the big psychologist coming through the door.

"We'd like to keep you here as long as possible. But not against your wishes, of course. You were shanghaied, not kidnaped." The left corner of his wide mouth pulled back in that slow, reassuring smile.

"I stand chastised. Now I've thought of it, though, I can hardly wait."

"The day after tomorrow? I want you to hear Caesar speak. Then I want to talk a good deal more."

"Early, the day after tomorrow." Then, little-boyishly, Jay hurriedly added a couple of reasons. "I'm getting tired of talking and being questioned. I feel like a talking animal in the zoo."

Ilaria nodded, smiling. "Julie?

"I figured it would occur to you sooner or later. Just because you think a little more deeply and carefully than most men of your time doesn't make you immune to love. That belongs to *all* times. Good luck and a lot of children."

Jay grinned. He'd met Ilaria's wife and five of his six children the night before. He turned to look out the window once more.

Beautiful. The elevated streets, with gyro-cars hurtling along ... the sky full of more winged gyros and planes ... the streets below full of happy, white-faced, white-clad people....

White-faced!

"Kevin, you avoided my question the day before yesterday. I've been almost afraid to ask you again. Why no Negroes?"

"It will be hard for you to accept, with your antiquated democratic ideas." Ilaria breathed a deep sigh. "Certain elements of dissension and unrest, Jay, are better eliminated. Coloreds have always bred both. People are just like that. Whites and yellows and tans and reds can get along, but not blacks."

Jay had gotten along with them all his life. "In ancient Rome there were slaves ..." he said, trying to understand.

"Not in this Rome. I said, better eliminated, Jay." Ilaria went to the window and looked down at the scene below. He explained:

"We exterminated them."

A hammer crashed down. A door slammed. A glass shattered. A siren screeched. A punch caught Jay in the solar plexus. Jay had experienced all these. Ilaria's flat statement was worse.

"Exter—No! Oh, No!" He swung around to face the big psychologist. Ilaria's usual smile was gone. He looked solemn and very grim.

"You weren't ready for it. I don't think we can discuss it. Just remember this: When you've a bunch of dogs and they all get along with one another except one, you don't leave them together and you don't try to keep them separated by a chicken-wire fence. It's too unpleasant. You get rid of the troublemaker."

During the night the rebel forces moved out of Tel Aviv and took over Israel. They captured the entire devastated Washington area, a series of ten cities ringing Rome, and hundreds of other key spots. The world's largest airbase at Madrid, Spain, was taken. Forces sent to the aid of the base defenders were met by an onslaught of their own planes. The troops didn't have a chance.

Dr. Montmorency Trumperi's Wave Disturber had been outlawed in 2001. The plans were carefully filed away and the machine's component parts junked. But the Disturber suddenly reappeared on the night of June 9, 2054, and world communications were stopped. Lamberti's scientists had come up with a counter-radio mechanism, of course, so that the Rebels were able to maintain contacts.

Louisville was not attacked. Lamberti and his men knew about the emissary from the past sheltered there, and informed their fifth columnists at Standiford they wanted both the Man From 1954 and Tribune Kevin Ilaria alive.

New York was attacked by land and air. Tokyo fell. Everywhere white flags with the blue Liberacione and the picture of a dove fluttered above smoking battlegrounds. Everywhere men were on the march.

When Tribune Kevin Ilaria stormed in twelve hours later, Jay noticed his friend was wearing his gun again. The cyanide pistol had not swung at his hip since the day of Jay's arrival. He was also surprised to note that Ilaria wore boots and carried a steel helmet under his arm.

There was a new quality in his voice. Brittle, static. The soft tones of the psychologist were gone.

Jay realized that this was Tribune Ilaria of the Forces, not Dr. Ilaria the psychologist.

"You sure you want to leave here tomorrow?" he demanded curtly.

Instantly Jay was on the defence. "I am," he said coldly.

Ilaria's smile looked forced. "I've been authorized to offer you a Sub-Tribunate in the Forces."

"What?"

"You've had experience. None of us have. You've been in actual combat, in the Air Force."

"Why? I don't—"

"War," Ilaria said simply. "Rebellion."

Jay stared at him. He couldn't think of anything to say.

Ilaria turned away. "Paradise. The Iron Hand. One religion and one language and all that. Utterly cock-sure. But ... we were wrong. They've been getting ready. Training and planning. Collecting men and arms. They began even before the empire was established."—Jay noticed he said empire rather than republic—"All this time they've been preparing and planning and ... waiting."

Jay was dumbfounded. "How big is it?"

Kevin Ilaria spread his hands. "Big enough. Their attack seems to have been simultaneous all over the world. Something like commando or guerrilla tactics. Quick, quiet attacks on a small scale."

He told Jay about the Tel Aviv incident and about Captain Spagnoletti and a half-track disappearing in the rubble in the Washington area and about intercontinental communication being shut off.

"Bomb 'em out," Jay said, without thinking.

"You don't bomb out fifth columnists, Jay.

"Last night they captured London and Tokyo and two-thirds of New York and they captured Lollabrigida airbase in Madrid. They're wearing PR uniforms and some kind of new uniform they've dreamed up. Most of them aren't even uniformed. It's a hell of a mess."

"How long do you think it'll take to quell the thing?"

"I have no idea. I'm to take command at Standiford Field. Rinaldi solved the saboteur problem ... it was Colonel Di Orio. Rinaldi and some of his boys caught the Colonel and a few of *his* men in the Radio Room on the special 'Liberacione' wave length."

"In irons?" Jay wanted to know.

"No. They put up a fight. They were killed."

"You're flying?"

"Doubt it. I'll be one of those behind-the-scenes men. Supposed to be valuable. Only in a mess like this you can't tell what's behind the scenes and what's front line. They're liable to start on Louisville next."

Ilaria hitched self-consciously at his gun-belt. He twisted his helmet around a couple of times before he set it gingerly on his head. He turned and opened the door and went out. His head came back in and said:

"I'm not sure it's the sort of thing you quell, Jay."

"Kevin! Wait! What'm I supposed to—"

He was gone.

Jay thought only a moment. Then he switched on the phone. At least intercom systems were still in operation. The clerk at the desk upstairs looked at him from the screen.

"This is the Man From 1954," Jay said, using the name by which everyone called him. "Stop Tribune Ilaria as he goes out."

In an instant Kevin's head appeared.

"I'll go with you. Shall I get my uniform before we go to Standiford or after?"

Ilaria grinned. "After," he said. "Grab the elevator and come on up."

This isn't your fight, Jay Welch, a voice told him as he opened the door. You don't even belong here, Jay Welch, the voice told him as he ran out into the hall. You're crazy to go to bat for these monsters, Jay Welch, the voice told him as he pushed the elevator button. You fought before for a bunch of people who didn't appreciate it one damned bit, Jay Welch. Remember about the Iron Hand and the Negroes, the voice told him as the doors opened and he stepped in. Remember you were shanghaied, it said, as the car shot upward and the bottom of his stomach felt as if it had been left behind. Remember you were going back to Duo Point and Herman's and Joe Scaccia's restaurant and Julie and tie and suit and Julie and the tight shoes and Julie and personal freedom and Julie and Jerry, the black guy you worked with and liked so well and Julie and the new Olds and Julie. Tomorrow you were going back.

The doors shot back. He stepped out on the roof.

"Mister Welcci?" said the clerk. "That's Tribune Ilaria's plane over there."

He pointed to the little PR ship marked with the three silver diamonds of a Tribune and the staff of psychology. Jay ran. Wind was whipping across the roof and their cloaks streamed out and fluttered. The three men came together.

"This is Commander DeVito, Jay. Commander, Jay Welch, The Man From 1954." The way Ilaria said it always made it sound capitalized.

They shook hands. They got into the plane and shot straight up and the city was a blur beneath them. In less than a minute the little flier dropped down faster than any elevator and landed at Standiford.

"Sergeant, Sub-Tribune Welcci needs a uniform. A—"

"Forty long," Jay suggested, then colored. Tunic and a hundred years made a difference in his size. He went with the supply-sergeant, who gave him a correct fit the first time—times *have* changed, Jay grunted—and fitted him with a helmet on the second try. He felt a tremor as he buckled on the pellet gun. With the cloak flapping about his heels and the gun banging his leg and the helmet biting his ear he ran to the elevator and down to the room Kevin had designated. The Tribune and Commander DeVito and five or six other officers were standing around a table in the steel-walled underground room.

Before them was a gigantic map. They looked up as Jay burst in.

"This is The Man From 1954," Ilaria said. There were hand-shakes all around that reminded Jay of fraternity rush. DeVito and one of the others wore wings. Jay wondered if that were still a pilot's insignia.

The red X's on the map, they told him, were places under attack. The blue ones were areas taken by the fast-moving rebels. He learned that the messenger-jet they'd sent to Rome—they were lost without their instantaneous push-button communications system—hadn't made it. More had been sent. Meanwhile they were on their own.

The nearest major battle was at Chicago, where Cocuzzi Flight Base was located. Ilaria despatched Commander DeVito and something like fifty jet fighters to Chicago. The other man was in charge of a group of B-90 Stratosonic bombers. They lifted their fists in stiff-armed salute and left.

"The rest of the ships will remain here, ready for instant take-off. I'll command interception. Sub-Tribune Rinaldi will command the base in case I have to go up.

"I can't understand why we haven't been jumped yet. We must assume they'll attack Louisville because of Standiford and the Time Building. They'll also be interested in you, Jay."

By 2:00 that afternoon Louisville had not yet been attacked. Abruptly at 1:59 world communications went into operation. Everyone turned on his television set, wondering if Caesar's talk would go on as scheduled.

It did. There was a screaming crowd before the Capitol. On the high balcony stood the Dictator. At his side stood Senator Chianti and around them were ringed Caesar's Pretorian Guards. The city was nearly empty of field soldiers. They had gone out to meet the insurgents.

"People of the Republic of Rome." The noise subsided as Caesar raised his hands and spoke.

"You have all heard of the revolt now in progress against us throughout the Empire."

Ilaria nodded at the Caesar's psychologically clever use of the word us.

"With your aid, my people, we can put a quick end to this treason. You have seen better than half a century of peaceful, successful government. These traitors and conspirators would attempt to overthrow our government and put an end to this peace ... this Peace of Rome.

"The world is now in a state of emergency. If you, my people, will bear with me through this period of crisis we will return to our world of peace and serenity once more."

Cheers. Wild applause.

"They believe him," Jay murmured.

Ilaria looked at him. "Of course," he said.

"For a long time our Empire has remained ..."

Caesar's face stiffened. The deep-set, weary eyes blazed and widened. His hand reached out for the railing. Then he stiffened again and was limp as the bursting pellet of sulphuric acid and potassium cyanide took effect.

Gaius Julius Caesar Imperator V fell.

There was uproar and clamor and shrieking.

Jay and Ilaria stood, staring, as the Pretorian Guards levelled their guns and became a solid, surrounding wall. The T-V cameramen were getting the scene of the century.

"Lamberti!" Ilaria bit out.

The Pretorian Prefect, his hands outspread, stood on the balcony over Caesar's body. The white cloak with Liberacione on it fluttered about him. A couple of Pretorians came out with an amplifier.

"Friends, Romans, Countrymen," said Farouk Lamberti.

"—every available long-range ship to Rome," Ilaria's brittle voice was hacking out orders. "Every one. Contact every other base while communications are still working!"

"... a noble man. But not the man to govern Earth. No, not he nor his government. I bring you a new government. I, Farouk Lamberti, long his best friend, have done this not to him, but for him. For you. The Earth was not meant to be governed by a system of—"

"Yes, I said bomb Rome."

Sub-Tribune Rinaldi smiled. "But Kevin, my friend, we can't bomb Lamberti just when he's getting a good start."

Jay looked up. Kevin Ilaria spun around. "What?"

"Never trust old friends, Kevin. Colonel Di Orio didn't. He surprised us in the Radio Room and we were forced to put him out of the way. Also remember this: all members of the Liberacione carry gamma pistols."

Rinaldi pulled out his gamma gun and shot Ilaria through the middle.

Jay was horrified. He forgot where he was and when he was and what he was doing. All he knew was that there was a cyanide gun at his hip and that this man had shot Ilaria. His gun came up and sputtered.

The pellet caught Rinaldi just under the chin and burst. Rinaldi collapsed.

"Had a—gamma gun—not ... deadly. Slow-acting ... radio-activity. Hardly ... burned me. Come on—we've got to ... get back to the—Time building."

"Oh, no we won't. You're hurt. We—"

"Don't argue. Sergeant! Saaarguunt!" Ilaria gasped at the exertion of shouting. The Centurion ran in.

"We've got to—get to the—Time building."

"Rinaldi shot the Tribune. Rinaldi was a traitor," Jay explained rapidly.

Ilaria's gun clicked and the Centurion shuddered back and fell through the door. The gamma burst from his pistol hit the wall.

"God! Is everyone a traitor?" Jay demanded of the Universe.

People are easily swayed. It didn't take them long to espouse the new cause. They were helped along in their decision by the Liberacione planes hovering overhead with loads of KCN-H2SO4 bombs. The whispering campaign Lamberti had carefully started about germ warfare helped, too. Those who didn't switch over rapidly were jumped by the new forces. Tribune Ilaria in Louisville, Kentucky, in America held out as long as he could. Then the bombers came. And the Tribune fled to the Time building.

The building shook. A table shivered and a lamp shattered. A jet fighter flew close by the window and the Centurion watched fearfully as it flipped on one delta wing and fired a tracer burst into a PR ship. The defender exploded in mid-air.

Ilaria looked twenty years older than the man who had smiled and welcomed Jay Welch to 2054. He and a young scientist were preparing the machine to send the man from 1954 back to his own time.

"You'll have to leave the gun here, Jay." Ilaria winced as he bent over a set of dials.

"I'd like to keep the uniform."

"All right. Does that do it, Doctor?"

The scientist nodded. He looked at Jay. "It's ready," he said.

"This switch sets everything in motion, doesn't it?" Ilaria asked.

"Yes. That's the final control."

"Then ... I'll do it. I'd like ... to say something to Jay before he leaves."

The scientist hesitated a moment, then shrugged and left. The Centurion went to the door. He was a young man and fanatically loyal.

"You all right, Tribune?"

Ilaria smiled. "I'm ... all right, Sergeant."

The Centurion nodded and left.

"Sit ... sit down in that chair, Jay, and do your best to relax."

Jay sat down. A bomber roared overhead. There was a blast nearby.

"What will you do now, Kevin?"

Ilaria shrugged. "Fight 'em 'til they come in and we're sunk. Then I'll join 'em. Why—why die a martyr's death?"

- 34 -

Of course, Jay told himself. Logical. But Kevin had been so convinced. So utterly sure. Now he looked and sounded like a disillusioned old man.

"Kevin, I'm not trying to rub it in. But—"

"I know what you're going to say. I was so sure. Paradise. I was a firm disciple. Convinced. I believed in all of it. I—thought it would last forever. The perfect government. A permanently *workable* government."

Jay sat quietly. Ilaria reached for the switch.

"For God's sake," came the voice of 1954, "what *is* the perfect workable government?"

Ilaria closed the switch and the light blinded Jay. He felt as if someone had slugged him in the stomach. Slowly the machine prepared to send him back one-hundred years. It warmed up like a jet on a runway.

The light faded and Jay opened his eyes. The building rocked. There was a terrific explosion and part of the steel wall buckled. Somewhere a woman screamed. A squadron of fighters hurtled past, spitting fire and death. A bomber fell, exploding as it crashed into a tall apartment building. Jay's stomach twisted and he knew he was on his way. Ilaria took his gun from his holster and calmly placed its ugly snout against his own face.

"... the perfect workable government?" Jay's question of a moment ago reached his ears as he began to slip back, minute by minute, picking up momentum. Ilaria's reply came dimly.

"There is none."

CPSIA information can be obtained
at www.ICGtesting.com
Printed in the USA
LVHW052355021121
702257LV00007B/902

9 789355 348517